LOVE
FOR
SLAUGHTER

POETRY BY

SARA
TANTLINGER

Published by Strangehouse Books
(an imprint of Rooster Republic Press)

Copyright © Sara Tantlinger
Cover by Nicholas Day

Printed in the USA.

www.strangehouseonline.com

"Sara Tantlinger has just sent a Valentine's present to your funeral. Seduction is a slaughterhouse in "Love for Slaughter" -- the first poetry book from this brilliantly evocative and subversively disturbing new horror writer -- a woman dead set on beheading Cupid and reminding us all how weird love really is. From the charm of the corpse to the beauty of butchery, Tantlinger's poems roil with dangerous desire and are relentlessly provocative -- satanically sultry stuff that you won't be able to stop reading."

Michael Arnzen, Bram Stoker Award-winning author of *Proverbs for Monsters* and *The Gorelets Omnibus*

"Sara Tantlinger's *Love for Slaughter* is full of dark moments of exquisite beauty. She is particularly adept at making even the bleakest of sentiments sound sensual and captivating. Full of clever wordplay, haunting rhythms, and excellent phrasing, Tantlinger's work is a must for readers who like their poetry with a side of sexy gloom."

K.W. Taylor, author of *The Curiosity Killers*

Acknowledgments

Thank you to ghosts, mine and those of other hearts, for bleeding yourselves into my veins and driving this collection to its completion.

Much warmth is extended to my two beta readers who read over *Love For Slaughter* first. Kathleen Taylor Kollman, thank you for the wonderful feedback. Your keen eyes and sense of poetry helped so much when I revised the collection. And thank you for swapping collections with me because it was such an honor to read your poetry. You are so, so talented.

And Dalton Lee Marks, thank you for such a raw reaction to the work. Your beautiful, analytical depth of feedback made me realize things about these pieces that I had not even thought of before. You're one of the first people who ever believed in my poetry, even when it was those ridiculous, slightly angsty pieces from our writer's café days. I am so grateful to have you as a friend.

Thank you to so many others who have supported me over the years. To Mike Arnzen who has been an incredible teacher and mentor both in regards to my poetry and prose. Your encouragement and ability to push me to always do my best has been such an important, driving force for me. Here's to many more poetry readings and kaffeeklatsches!

To my mom, Cassie, and my sister, Michelle, who have always been supportive of my writing even if it's all darkness, blood, and death. Love you both!

To my wonderful friends (you know who you are), and I can't thank you enough for your support. It means the world.

And to Nick Day and StrangeHouse Books for giving this collection a home. From the bottom of my bloody little heart, thank you.

"You said I killed you--haunt me then. The murdered do haunt their murderers. I believe-- I know that ghosts have wandered the earth. Be with me always--take any form--drive me mad. Only do not leave me in this abyss, where I cannot find you! Oh, God! It is unutterable! I cannot live without my life! I cannot live without my soul!"

— Emily Brontë, Wuthering Heights

LOVE FOR SLAUGHTER
Sara Tantlinger

Table of Contents

Alouette

She likes a little horror in her romance
blood simmering on her lips
when you kiss her, and she lives for
the bruise, bite, blister of love's rhythm.
You'll think she's beautiful
when she tears you to pieces and sings
Alouette, gentille Alouette,
while ripping shreds of skin from you,
her bird. She will have you in a cage

pluck layers of your soul away.
She'll lure you into her night, trap
your mind until you're driven insane,
almost hate her, but in the end you will
always fall in love with her darkness.

She will open you up,
trace the lines of your heart
like wrinkles on a palm
and tell you if you live with her by your side
or die alone. She will tear out your veins,
stick them between her teeth
to keep your smoky flavor on her tongue.

Declare your love
when you fall asleep,
your back to her, she'll sink teeth
into your spine. With love in her heart,
she will destroy you.
When she cuts your throat,
you'll thank her. She'll save your blood
in jars until it's time
to recreate you because darling,
fairy tales start with once upon a time
the girl got the prince,
but in end,
she lived happily ever after
    with the monster.

Butchery

Tell me all the terrible things
you did so I can love you more
so I can want you with clarity,
no boundaries allowed.

I want to have you with carnage
on my hands, poison on my lips,
bruises on your neck, thighs, wrists
from my love like butchery, kisses
that slaughter, eyes that consume.

Tell me how we will murder each
other at the end of this affair, how
love is killed because we were too
raw, because we loved too bloody.

I sharpen my knife. You sharpen yours.
I want your *folie à deux, our madness
shared by two, a delicious psychosis*
where I scream, "I love you, kill me."

And you echo, *I love you, kill me.*

Nyctophilia

I was in love with Night,

the way she whispered
into my splintered heart
and told me someone
who consumed
as much darkness
as I did would either
become a poet
or a murderer.

I decided to be both.

I killed who I loved
without question
or concern
because Night
promised me
that killing love
is the most
poetic.

When I saw you,
Night grew jealous.
How could I not
love you?
The sliver of the moon
is weaved between
your spine,
inside your muscles.

I want to rip
those slivers
out of you
suck them down
into my marrow,
and capture the bats
in your throat
with my lips.

I long to cut you and see
the stars in your veins,
to know if you bleed
their light. I want to find
the constellations
hiding in your blood,
and scatter them across
Night so that she may love
us as we love her,

before the sun arrives
chars us into ashes,
murders our poetry.

Heart for a Corpse

You looked at me as if to say, *how dare you swallow my heart?*
but yours is not the first to be devoured by my overeager appetite.
If you understood how hungry someone born by loneliness
can get to be, maybe you wouldn't blame me for removing
your teeth while you slept, for sliding my hand into your mouth,
down your throat, and plucking your heart out of you like uprooting
roses from a neighbor's garden at night. Maybe you would
sympathize with my ache to stuff that heart between my shaking lips,
to feel its warmth slide down my throat because it has been so
long since something warm and beating lived beneath my skin.

Black Ties and Atom Crushing

You in the black tie,
me in the scarlet dress.
It's a scandal,
a cliché,
and a moment to be.

So we be.
And you're smiling
softly, like feathers,
but I don't want softness
for this moment.

I want hard and aching,
your breathing swallowed
by my lips, and I taste
every molecule of your being.
I want your atoms.

The way I absorb you,
consume and create
through atom crushing.
I remake you, reinvent
the man into my kind of monster.

The Filth in You

I bathe demons in sunlight
and create you from their dirt.
I stitch your filth together
with the hair of broken corpses,
feed you blood of the infected,
and steal dying gasps of sinners
to breathe life into you, my darkling.
I am your god, and I create you
in my image--scarred and wicked.

Obeyed

Mouths burn like cigarettes
inhaling dusted deceptions
cremating telltale signs
because malice tastes
like sugared lemons on my tongue
and I long to suck the sour embers
from your teeth until my lips blister.

Convince me you deserve to suffer,
I will bring you satisfaction.

Heaven should obey us.
We are instruments of the divine,
and confession comes first, but so
do I when your head is between my
thighs after you burnt butterfly wings
and kept the ashes on your tongue.

Convince me you deserve satisfaction,
I will bring you suffering.

But this is okay because I want all
the worst parts of you. You're the drug
in my brain and when you dissolve
into me I see the colors on the murderer's
canvas. My heartbeat is electric inside
the spilled gasoline you poured down my throat.

Convince me you deserve a bright world,
I will bring you scarlet hell.

Notch Post

The razor of your tongue
is a demon I wish to tame
in darkness, unable to see
the blood flowing from cuts
you have carved into my body
with your sharp mouth.

Serenades for Dead Lovers

I heard the song you wrote about me, about the sick thing we call love,
but you painted our crimes
with fluttering verses
that claim
      we are forever.
There is blood between the bridge leading into our chorus.
You can't write a tune as sinful as us
and expect sugared melodies.
We turned acrid when I stabbed you

and you pushed me down on the cement.
Our cadence is broken
      bones, not soft touches.
Is that the song of lovers?
You can tell me you're clean now, but don't act like you don't miss
the dirt of us.
Lust may make you crazy, but love will make you kill.
Didn't we prove that with the pile of dead bodies around our bed?
Go on, serenade me

with that fake song, croon out your love and kill
me at the end, slip into me
      like the louse you are
because I think you've filled my heart with bees
and my tongue is venom.
I want my spit to seep into your pores until you swell and turn purple
from all that poison flooding your veins.
Pretend I'm your daytime melody,
but I know you're meant to be sung in the dark.

My fingertips trace every note of you, flat and sharp, lined and curved.
When you sleep,
I hum that tune softly
and draw the word *murder* across your back.
I break
      into full refrain when my hand
glides up to wrap around your throat, and I ask you
to sing me your song baby,
scream it out loud.

Apocalypse Girl

She fucks like velvet
and her spit holds
a whiskey taste. She lost
her soul in the woods
where she hung priests
from tall, ancient oaks.
She swallows silver bullets
and dances with angels
before slitting their
throats with her serpent
teeth. She doesn't have
friends, just a champagne
voice that lures anyone
near her. She carries my life
between her fangs,
and I follow, helplessly
in love with a girl
named Doomsday.

Muse Incarnate

My muse, how shall I write the story of you?

First there is ink, spurting cherry colors
as I slide my knife into your ribcage,
unlocking organs to create a scarlet font.

You shudder from the slow intimacy
of my teeth hovering over you before
I bite the aorta and swill the flavor
on my tongue until my gums are sticky
with the metallic taste of you.

I swallow each thump of your heart
as it fades from you and is reborn
to thunder inside of me. My skin
pulses in murmurs that echo your voice.

I write you as timeless, living incarnate
inside my veins where we beat eternally.

Unstitched

The seams of you
are sutured tightly,
but I know where
your scars hide.
I remember serrated
wounds against
my tongue, tasting
like ocean salt.
I will pull you apart,
your strings unlaced
and your blood
like waves rushing
into my mouth
as I unstitch you.

Letters On Your Spine

It wasn't always like this. I didn't always used to keep my eyes open when he kissed me, when he slid into me and sighed in a surrender I can no longer remember. Now he crawls up toward me and folds against my body like an accordion, up and down, and I count the circles of plaster on the bedroom ceiling.

We're liars. We can't be trusted, not even with each other.

It's become a ritual. After he falls asleep, his back toward me, I trace the word *killer* against his spine with my fingertips, one slow letter at a time dancing across his sleeping skin. Tonight is different. Tonight I know what all the letters stand for.

K

where did the key go? The one that slotted us together months ago when we still understood each other? I think the lock is inside your mouth and I'm too tired of your guarded tongue to go searching.

I

I can die, I'm alive. I'm a person sick of cutting my own skin just to show I'm alive. I'll drown in my own bleeding to show you I can die, too. I can die.

L

love asked me to swallow my own heart. I obeyed.

L

I said love. What crueler word is there? You're keeping me on my grave, waiting like a child for the sun to rise on Christmas. You were supposed to be my better half, not the one to bring all this hate and darkness to my surface.

E

did you expect this to be easy, to teach a wicked girl to behave? Turn me on and I'll destroy you.

R

his spine snaps and there is red. Red, red everywhere.

Spider Heart

Your heart crawled
from your mouth
on skinny legs
skulked toward my lips,

I swallowed
it down
and dreamt of flies,
diseased and buzzing

demanding blacker, stickier love
until tiny wings cling like cobwebs
to my knees
and I leave a sticky trap
where ever I roam.

You make my bite sharper,
the curve of my smile colder,
and you know I am at my best
when I kill right after sex.

Thank you for the malevolence,
I'll wear it well,
beneath the red hourglass
of my spider heart.

Froth

Let's count the bodies around us
as if they were stars, glowing
and beautiful, full of life,
not buried below our feet
trembling in earth's cold tomb.

Let's brew blood tonight,
half mine and half yours,
mixed together in smoldering
gurgles of a raspberry froth,
and we'll feed each other
with the life of our selves.

Shards in Your Eyes

You kiss me and I'm pouring wineglasses
over our mouths. No, not wine,
just broken
        off shards
from celebratory crystal

happy anniversary

glass falls down our faces
as our lips meet,
and I wonder if devotion will cut us
or if we'll make it unscarred,

but what fun is romance without blood?

Especially our kind of adoration,
how it ticks
        the wrong way
steady your palms and see
if this backward love
speaks affection in reverse
like the words of the devil,

or something far worse.

Lungs on Fire

Hello fire,
blistering inside your mouth.
This kiss tastes like sin
and I know
Satan watches me from inside
your copper eyes.
Your name scorches
me outside in. Strike a match against
my heart, see how it bleeds?

My scarlet trail thickens to gel
from the slow burn
of your life slinking
inside, like I've swallowed coals
and they grew tiny centipede legs
to creep down my throat.

The singe of you blackens my bones
and rains ashes in my veins
from the smoking demise
of my lungs that could no longer
support me screaming your name.

Darling, I am on fire.
I am dead in your arms,
Kiss me one last time,
your wet tongue
on my burnt flesh,
remind me why I gave all I had
just to know for one moment,
the fire raging inside of you.

Carolina

They never think we know, she whispers.
This might be a dream,
but the broken beats of her heart are real.
She is an outline,
blurred around the edges.
I can't see her face, but I bet she's pretty,
big eyes and a sweet laugh. You have a type.

She is here with a warning, but I already
know the truth about you.
I found out first, but now she
is almost me, and the world is still asleep.
I ask, *where did you come from?*
Why did he find you when he had me?

She holds up a faint hand, *almost.*
I don't know what to say
because the broken heartbeats I hear
are not hers, she did not fall
that far into your chaos.
Those beats are mine. I can't kill Carolina
or your others, lost wandering in heather plants,
not knowing of my existence.

You keep me so hidden,
but your flesh cannot hide, your blood
cannot disappear, not until I find you
slice that soft neck and drain you
upside down until every lie is a red puddle
drooling from you to the hungry ground.

You never did learn to clean up your messes.

Mirror Me

Sometimes I am sorry
that I loved you wrong,
that it was not,
(is not)
love for the right reasons

I want to apologize
for the meanness
that lives inside
my cold tongue,
my rageful heart

but despite the poison
dripping from my teeth
and despite your apologies

I cannot forgive you

the truth is
I want you to hurt

I want to leave you in pieces
shred you up,
grant you heartbreak so raw
that you will never
let anyone close again
never let anyone
touch you, love you, heal you

pain, my final gift to you
wrapped up inside a mirror
reflective of my wounds

feel free to break the glass
and cut your own throat

Eye Candy

I make your eyes
burst like blueberries
between my teeth,
soothing my tongue
with the cool juice
of your navy irises.
The cracks of my
lips stick together
with delicate drops
of cobalt nectar,
making me a glutton
for such candied ruin.

Funhouse

There's something wrong here
in the way we hold one another
at night like secrets, like the space
between our bodies created
a monster from our curved shadows.

We are sinking into the chasm
of cruel affection. Clawing at each
other's skin as we slide around our
funhouse love where the mirrors shatter
and cut through our gaping mouths.

Loving you is like swallowing
spoons, choking on their bent bellies,
letting the handle slide through my
throat until it protrudes and there's
a lever jutting out from my neck.

Pull the handle, give it a try, see what
kind of demonic prize spews from
my jaws for you to win after we kiss
because in the end I am going to fall
in love with the monstrous version of us.

I will promise on the ocean's every grain
of sand to destroy you before our lurid
game ends, before the freaks arrive
with questions about what we created,
and ask why we let the beast out of the cage.

Crawl to Me

He told me he liked me
on my knees, enjoyed
watching me crawl across
the room and make my way
over to where he waited
for me to sink my teeth
into his naked thighs
and suck the blood away
until he was dizzy, until
he pulled me away,
kissed my bloodstained
mouth and got off,
but this time I kept my lips
pressed against him. I bit his
tongue, trapped it between
my teeth and shook roughly
like a dog with a chew toy.
The muscle ripped.
I pinched his nose shut
and cut off his air.
He swallowed down his
tongue and choked on the
bleeding, squirming worm.
I stood up and watched his
body twitch on the floor,
violent little shakes of agony
as I walk away.

I crawl to no one.

Opponent

She loved him best
because of a single
ridiculous day when he
held the blue plastic bag
up and asked her to keep
it over his head until he
stopped breathing.

"Only if I can join you,
suffocate myself too,"
she said. And the man
replied, "No. The world
would then be deprived
of your beauty."

She loved him most then,

and their love grew
into a sick suicidal
kind of affair
where they stayed
alive like it was
a challenge.

She was never quite
sure if she was
betting on him,
or if she was
his greatest adversary.

Four years, he knocked
at her heart. 1,460 days
he stayed on her mind,
haunted her like a living ghost,
and she regretted, always,
not pulling the plastic bag
down over hazel eyes,
sinful lips, over the neck
she once had her palms
pressed against.

34

She promised never again
not to honor
an enemy's request for death.

Atrophy

I inhale you
when I have you under me,
breathing deep
to get you in my blood,
but you're always there,
my lingering virus

between these sheets
is where love atrophies
because we kill desire,
shred through
monstrous intimacy

a shaking body is left

the wounds are infected
and we paint over them
with pastels, but even after
the death of romance,
desire never leaves.

Unsaid

What have we done, to our hearts, to each other?

You have hurt me again and I am trying to care, but numbness pervades my body. The light of affection between us has smeared like fireflies against our palms. We attempt to reconcile, but what you call harmless, I call a bullet.

Our excuses are false. I could choke on the letters and offer you a Joker smile over this mad love, baby because you can't adore a girl like crazy and expect her to stay sane. I fed you accusations and thought this is it, this is why falling in love feels like dying.

You give parts of yourself away to someone and they scatter you, let your pieces float down the river. You try to put yourself back, but your puzzle of a body is sodden. You'll never be sharp again. You fell in love and all your edges turned to pulp. You are not whole.

Who are you now?

I begged you to show me some shame, but you loved your dishonesties more than you loved me.

Let me tell you about the quiet of it all, the way our blood pumps after you've gotten off inside me and

(fuck that August love)

we try to figure out if we're really meant to be, or if this is just loneliness in a mask.

I'd like to think you'd only get so furious at someone you really care for, but I've never been taught this lesson before. I'm standing still with the apologies I loathe, cringing as they hatch like spider babies on my tongue, but I swallow the unsaid words down and let spite ooze through my bloodstream until I evolve into the kind of monster worthy of the furious word-creatures inside the cellar of my gut.

You wanted to take love like big gulps into your lungs. I was just trying not to disrupt the air around me. I'm giving more and you keep taking, which is fine because I want you to have me, but now I'm empty except for the squirming sludge of anguish that moves through my veins.

That mess is all I have to give back. I will give until it devastates you, until your bones blacken beneath the heat of my heartache and you burn from the inside out. All those kept secrets will pour out of you, and I'll touch my fingertips to them, and maybe then I can finally, and sincerely, love you.

Countdown

You are the bomb ticking in my brain
and here comes the fuse for detonation

five,
were we ever good enough to love like this?
four,
I guess it doesn't matter, so long as you surrender
three,
your clock is running backward darling, and the forest is on fire
two,
come to me before your body combusts, before flames melt your hair
one,
your bones will sing my name when I crawl inside your skin to rot

zero
the inferno screams our story as we melt inside its darkness

Death for My Darling

You are something I know so well,
I've forgotten I even know it at all.
You are the past, and I'm desperately
seeking to unravel your buried secrets,
the ones you've hidden in my brain.

I've traveled through all these lifetimes,
and you've been a shadow in every one.

I always kill you in the end, right before
the turn of a new century, but this time
I am cornered. You've dug my grave.

I know you'll destroy me without softness
for all the knives I have buried in your skin.
My coffin sings to me, and you know the
tune because you wrote my death march.

So please, love me when you kill me.

Keep Me, Haunt Me

Let us be toxic,
let us be damned and bring one another to ruins.
Cut my throat and glutton yourself
with the taste of my blood, devour my heart into your belly, hoard my soul
against your ribs.

Dine on my lustful smiles, get lost in the storm of my eyes, tell every tree
how you love so fiercely you will never let the girl go. Be selfish and keep
me, every twisted, soured part.

Be greedy. Lock me up and paint my portrait on prison walls. Make me your
need, your want, your sin. Invade my senses as only the disease of love can
and let our passion run through this world as a leviathan of chaos.

Scorch me down like a candle,
smother my flame beneath your fingertips, scald your skin on the heat of me.

When I die, follow me through the veil and haunt me in purgatory where I
am devoid of your physical being. Be my ghost and make me cry with your
sharp words, make me feel something again in this betwixt place of the
afterlife. If I get lost in purgatory's trees, burn the whole place away and
follow me through the ashes into the pure black nothingness below.

Let us sit in darkness and trace the outline of one another's faces in this place
of only shadows. If you love me then follow me, haunt me, keep me hurting,
wanting, and alive in the dark, but never let me go.

Vampire Violets

He looks at me with violet eyes
and the stars commit suicide.

I find no peace here,

but I pretend to love a cold heart
under a sky of shadows and nothing
more. The moon still sings to me.

He looks at me with violet eyes
and the lust will drive me mad.

I am his pale prodigy, dancing wild
and offering my wrist for him to
bite me, to drink me up because the
stars are dead and I still crave love.

Hell's Hallelujah

When I heard her Hallelujah,
I fell like a shot down bird
from my home in the sky.
My body plummeted
through the core of the planet
and into Hell's belly.
The Devil did not speak to me
until after I asked if this
headfirst skyrocketing out of Heaven
was what they called love?

The Devil tended to my wounds in silence.
A black tree stood in the middle of her Hell,
grown from a molten pool of blood.

She kissed me beneath the tree and I knew
she'd always be the scream caught in my throat.
My heart ruptured in want for her to bury me.
I ached to have her plant my bones
in the ground, for my purity to create
the beautiful something her song yearned for.

I gave her my soul
and she fed it to the black tree,
to its heinous roots.
It changed from shadow to white hope.
I knew from the first moment
when I heard her tune that I'd give
the last of my grace
to the Devil I love so that she may smile
in peace, even if she can't see me,
but how could I mind that she's looking down
to the roots where I am buried?

I was the one to fall in the first place.

To Be Strange

To be strange is to be in love.
At one moment I want to kiss you,
slide you up against the door,
make you stutter and sigh.
At another moment I want to kill you,
slide my knife along your Adam's apple,
make you shiver and bleed against my skin.

Second Skin

You left your dead skin cells
on my sheets
wrapped around the scent
of sweat and cologne

and your lifeless particles of hair
remain on the pillowcase
where you laid your head too close
to mine

I hope you don't come looking
for what you lost

you won't find them here

I roll around on my bed
like a dog rubbing
its fur raw
against road kill,
tongue lolling out
and senses on fire
as I absorb you into my pores

I wear the dust of your dead atoms
like a second skin
until I am with you again.

Assassination of Sunlight

I put the sun in my mouth and swallow it.
I leave you with nothing but my night
hoping you feel as I do, vindicated under
the stars, like getting away with Earth's
murder as we slice love into dead slivers.

I'll lead you to the well, to the wishbone I stole.
We can each pull one end, watch it break during the witching hour.

Our hearts have been singed like spider legs
crawling across burning bulbs. We are arachnid
bodies left without limbs, without transportation
from web to sustenance, so I swallow this light too.

I watch you wriggle your twitching, legless body
home, if home still exists for something as defiled
as you. In the end if you get too lost I'll ask you
to cut me open and spill these lights I've drunk.

I'll guide you away from my own tornado of ruin, lead you
into the woods to curl up and die alone like a wounded dog.

I will be the wolf in your heart
howling as you perish
until my lights fade.
I will find you in the next life
where we grasp the twisted ways
we fell, and how we will always fall
in love
in every life,
until our lights are scattered into stars
and our names are constellations swallowed by the sun.

Match Mouth

I wrote your name across my arm,
as if seeing the letters I loved to soak
in my brain could bring me closer to you,
but you stayed gone. The letters taunted me.

I tried to scratch them out, to slash across your
name with the pocketknife you left behind
and have my blood smear the letters together,
but my blackened heart remained in mourning.

I wanted to wash you away, to end my suffering
by scalding my skin into an angry, bubbling pink,
to rinse you down the drain, but again it did not
work, and you are still hiding under my flesh.

You're haunting every inch of me like a slithering,
cancerous snake, hissing in my brain as your tail wraps
around my windpipe, daring me to speak your name
before you plant heavy tumors inside my lungs.

So I drink gasoline until it sours my stomach, until I'm
ready to vomit and collapse. I think of how you fueled
me with acetone lies and tried to love me with coals.
I strike the match, hold it to my mouth, and swallow fire.

Peccavi

I love you
because I have no right to,
and because you are not mine,
but I want you anyway.

I want your brutality sliding
into me like a secret. I want
you in an overpriced hotel
room we've booked solely
for the purpose of our misdeeds.

I want the lights off because we
are shadows sleeping with sin
and do not deserve the sun's gaze.
We are silhouettes in moonlight.

I love you
because we made this choice,
and because we are damned
to the darkness we created.

Love for Slaughter

Happy anniversary. Blow out the candles.
Did you wish for death? For that black-winged creature called Love to crawl
out of your eyes, steal you away, and take you into the darkness?
Did you take Love to the butcher and have her slaughtered?

I'm having that dream again where I behead you, hang you upside down, and
bathe in the waterfall of your blood. You rush through me like I'm absorbing
a sunset. Even then you try to kill me.

We have hidden emotions beneath dynamite, and I am tired of the pile
stacking higher. I will stand here and light the fuse because I know the
explosion will etch out the hole in our future. Betrayal has sucked us through
the void and we've painted love black, like engulfing oil into our lungs.

Our hearts are tar pits full of snakes. I am trying to charm their way out with
a serenade, but all you want to hear are songs of venom to feed the serpents'
fangs.

The malice taints your mouth, but when you're gone I miss those hell-
flavored kisses. Without you, I am selling shadows to demons and picking at
the places on my body where your fingertips lingered, scratching them until
the scabs turn to scales.

Love is deathless.

You try to melt it like rubber burning into fresh asphalt, but that road is
paved on a path for your funeral procession, and I'm wearing all black
beneath my skin. You can't kill Love because Love is me, and there's a
graveyard inside my skull.

Your name has been carved onto a tombstone since our first kiss. And when
you fucked me, I dug your grave. Don't pretend you don't like this cemetery
sex and bed of bone because the only thing I want more than you, is to
devour our wickedness until your intestines twist out of your flesh, slide up
your body and wrap you in a cocoon of all that digested lust.

Go ahead and take me to the slaughterhouse. I dare you.

Paramour

"Do you love him?" Her hands
are on my waist. Her hair is
a mint perfume, drawing me near.
He spelled my name out in leaves,
I tell her. She says it isn't the same.
"The wind will come. The rain."

He calls me angel.
"You are full of sin."
He gives me dreams.
"You crave nightmares."

I sigh. She is the ice I long
to hold in my mouth.
"He is not you. He does not
hold your soul, not like I do."

Her lips are sweet poison
against my own, and I fall
into her world of darkness.

Or Something

Last night I gathered pebbles,
perfect ones without a blemish
shaped like smooth, rounded
discs in shades of brown, green,
and blue -- the colors of the earth
to represent the way our love
is a part of nature, of the world.

Tonight I toss those stones
at your house, sharp raps
against glass until you wake up
and look outside, see me
standing on the grass, shivering
in a thin gray jacket as the wind
shakes the fringe of your bangs.

You open your window to either
tell me to come and see you or
shout at me to go away, but I
don't listen. I still have rocks
to throw, I still have wounds
to cause, so open your mouth
and I will feed you pebbles.

They will grind against your teeth,
break your molars, stain your tongue,
and catch in your throat until you
choke, until your voice stops haunting
my dreams and no longer do I hear
your demand to *be more romantic,*
toss pebbles at my window, or something.

Incurable

We stand beneath the moon,
me with apple-red cheeks
from the winter wind,
you with black gloves
and warm breath that blows
hazelnut kisses
from the coffee we drank.

I pretend for a moment
imagine we are not designed to fail,
that the snow is sugar
and the gold band around your finger
is fake, a chocolate ring
you wear as a joke.

I pretend we do not share
a mutual longing
to be destroyed

is this guilt?

We crave obliteration, to be left
in street gutters
like underfed cats,
feral and clawing one another
until love dissolves
into such strong grief
that I think I've mourned you
all the time
you've been living beside me.

Vices

I heard you whispering my name
that night in the rain, but the drugs
were closer and the liquor too.
I took all the wrong pills until you
loved me again, until my taste buds
felt like I was eating rabbit hearts.
I could lick your face and leave blood
trails for you to remember me.

I'm trying to get you out of my system,
but how do you wash permanent marker
out from under your skin? I'm just a thief
building coffins to put your stolen memories in,

but the dark church of your mind does not fit.

The silence
between winter days falls like dewy drops,
and the world grows ashen
with an anthem of bones ground to white powder.
We named the coldness after ourselves.

Is it too strange now with your spit in my throat
and my knee between your thighs?

We're creating
madness from sanity

and lust from the love we denied,

so taste the toxins placating the addict in me.

We're both greedy leeches getting fat from the blood
of each other. Repeat the vices, feel them slick
and biting, note when your tongue touches the tip
of your teeth, and fall
down, down, down

the sinner's rabbit hole with me.

Red Tree

The wolf man sleeps beneath her,
his Red Riding girl. She grows in
the dirt, scarlet bones protruding
from her ribcage, wild little branches
decorated with the unwound thread
of her skin like skeletal leaf strings.

The cherry moon illuminates the teeth
of his heart, showing this wide-eyed
lover is nothing but a cur with growling
throat and hungry tongue, waiting to
devour Red's organs that blossom from
her bark when the seasons change.

Cardiac

There is life inside her
kicking a beat against skin
warm beneath flesh
nestled tight.
She wants you out,
you do not belong inside
you do not deserve her life.
You are sick,
and she made you that way.
The doctor watches
mouth covered by a mask,
but those eyes
look at her as if she will be
devoured, and she knows
what he will do
to her body if the procedure
kills her.
He assures her this will be fine
as he holds a knife,
does not blink. She places hands
across her chest
where you thunder
inside
and she whispers
cut it out of me
this wretched beating.
Cut it out.

She closes her eyes.

Fateful Unfaithful

I wander the streets like a vagrant bee,
buzzing from lover to bed, bed to lover
in a cycle down the highway until I find
home again, and home is where you wait
so faithfully that I want to rip out my hair
and braid together a noose for your neck.

Yell at me, hit me, hurt me, anything but
this silent tolerance of my disloyalty.
Bash my head against the fireplace corner
where we sat and held hands, slice through
every inch of my skin with the hunting
knives we bought together last winter.

Suffocate me in the bed where we slept,
argued, laughed, and slid against one
another's heated bodies. Bury me beneath
the dim streetlamp where we first kissed,
anything but this quiet acceptance.
Kill me, but never stop fighting for me.

Quarry

I clutch
at your absence
like a starving cat
who has just caught
the squawking
delicate cardinal
between his sharp
quivering jaws and
it is you whom
I devour.

Petal Drained

Her skin went deep, and he was drowning
between all that bone and lean muscle.
Every time she whispered, *I love you,*
he carved an X into his palm as a reminder.

She blew death-kisses, like a summer
dandelion painted black. He tried to make
a wish before her invisible petal of a mouth
brushed against his cheekbone, but she
was quicker. His eyes seared, blistered,
and bled teardrops down his love-struck face.

Those September lips drove him to insanity
as he thought about her broken under him,
neck crooked and eyes open, his spine
singing out a tune of what her corpse-worms
would feel like crawling through his eyes,
under his nails, all the way into his skull,

and between his muscles, their tiny sharp teeth
latched on like leeches, draining everything
that was not needed to know the very last
intimate memory of his black-dandelion girl.

Arsenic Lust

The distance between you and I
is withering, succumbing inside
desperation laced with intrigue.

We are lust with an arsenic flavor,
the kind that comes in an ocean-blue
bottle and beckons calm surrender.

I question if you watch silently,
but the deafening quiet between us
would be easier if you didn't carry
a cigarette scent, making me wonder
what else I can get you addicted to.

Composer

I want to be the one left
when your life ends
and your bones collapse.
Only I will remain
to remember you
and I will choose
how to craft you
from my memories.
Do I make you better?
Darker and unforgiving?
You will be as my words
compose you to be.

I create you.

Riven

He didn't know what to do when
she left. His every muscle, organ,
vein, had been cemented together
by the love she'd granted him.

To be rid of her essence was the only
answer. He started from the outside,
a lighter under his hand to burn off the
fingertips that once caressed her face.

He touched his eyelashes, the ones that
had softly brushed against her cheeks,
and plucked them from his eyelids
one-by-one as he chanted *she loves me not.*

Yet she remained under his skin, like a
tapeworm sliding through him. When he
recalled the wet warmth of being inside her,
he swallowed bleach in desperate gulps.

As the chemicals broke down in his body, he
retreated inside the layers of himself, let his
muscles, organs, veins disappear until he was
pure again, until his cells dissolved and he
was but stardust once more, and nothing of
his remains knew a single memory of her.

The Lies He Loved Me With

The lies he loved me with
cut his teeth when the words
slithered beneath his gums
and across his tongue,
bleeding my name onto
the cracks of his lips.

The letters dripped like melting
candles from mouth to skin
until the lies he loved me with
became all he could splutter
in dying breaths
as I fed him razors,
my sharp little truths.

Becoming

He wants him, but he knows
this love is like trying to catch
a dropped knife, but the other
man does not care. After all,
he is gripping the blade's handle.

Wolfish hunger holds them,
aches inside rumbling guts,
but tonight the moon invites
their power-play to bathe
in silver beams. Tonight
a different man struggles between
them. They gut him together,
takes bites of his throat and heart.

They love with crimson starvation
and bathe in blood glimmering
coal-colored in the moonlight.
One man is savior
and one is devil,
but differences disappeared
when they tore a human to wet ribbons
and slicked their skin with his death.

Tonight they are equally drenched
in warm gore, devoid of sanity
before they fall from the bluff
and ask the ocean to drown them in a lullaby.

One last blood song.

Electric Nerves

Shocked awake
by your static
fingertips,
flipping through
the switches
of my memories
like electrocution
to the heart.
You make me
convulse
until I am nothing
but twitching nerves.

Hymn for the Wicked Angel

Self-sacrificing masochist,
my contradiction who stands
in the dark, protecting me
from demons, yet I rip
your wings apart in my teeth
and use your crippled feathers
to floss between my bones

because that is where monsters
have nestled inside me and left sick
babies to hatch, to swim in my blood
and defile my veins until I am
recreated in their putrid image,

but I am you, my faithless seraph,
my wicked hymn sung
only at night where every touch
is fire, where your haloed eyes
lose their light and we slide
in sweat to that same old ballad,

and the demons lurking in shadows
stay far away enough to watch,
and the demons in my blood
are calm from an angel's sinful touch.

Kiss Me Before You Kill Me

Blunt nails leave crescent
shapes on your back when
your palms spread my legs
and your lips find my thighs.

The way you leave blisters
where your mouth has been
whispering scandals into my
skin makes me arch higher,
searching for your cruel bite.

The tip of your tongue leaves
lines of lies along my body
that make me crave the death
you promised long ago,

but here we are, caught between
sheets, stuck together with kisses,
and dreaming of suffocating one-
another where we rest our heads
every night, burnt out from lust.

Our brains twitch from the unfinished
kill, and our hearts hammer, knowing
next time we'll either repeat our pattern,
or leave these sheets in crimson stains.

Nocturnal Language

My mouth is ancient
and her name between
my lips is a curse
from the old world
where we all fell in love
between barbwire teeth
and uncivil tongues.

She is chaos no longer
spoken because her name
shines black fire into lungs
and turns bones to charcoal.
She leads me to shorelines,
fills my stomach with stones
and I am weighed down
to drown in her night-ocean body.

She told me to treat my feelings
like a final story, before
I can no longer understand
the way letters twist, before
they stumble from lips
like cricket legs drunk
on saliva, forgetting how
to walk, how to sing.
But I will never forget.

She is permanent in my skull,
her heart feeds my thoughts,
her tongue gives me words
to throw across the darkness,
and her screams will forever
be my language of the night.

Pink Caterpillars

Do you remember those afternoons
where I plotted my death as we swayed
on whining swing sets with shaking bolts?
I talked in abstractions and you added
details, the right height to stand from
if I tied the noose and jumped, the vertical
direction to cut the vein in my arm,
the way my skull would burst
and leak wet brain drops from my head
like a rain of pink caterpillars.

All those curved conversations
and you never calculated the gasps
that would leave your mouth
when I pressed our favorite quilt,
the one with blue stitches and silver
squares, against your face until you
stilled, so I could watch you
be dead and hear your silence before
I laid me down next to you, poison
in hand and a craving on my lips.

Rope Maker's Dance

I want to hang you
from a noose
made of your distorted
entrails, circling
your neck
and suffocating
the vocal cords
that fed me saccharine lies
over vinegar truths.

I want to watch you swing
down in a rope maker's dance
before silence waltzes
with you into the nothingness.

Sonata of the Slain

I pulled you toward me, and the sky grew
jealous. I caught you between my thighs
and you shook like thunder, but your storm
consisted of soft breaths and drawn out
laments. I conducted your gasps, and you
became my symphony. We moved to a
sweating rhythm and composed our song
in the dark. We never asked for light.

Your fingertips on my tongue taste like
ash. I'll suck the powder up into the roots
of my teeth, like rain for watering the garden
of my gums, but we never cared much for
flowers. The tulips outside our bedroom
were starved, swallowed by weeds. We sent
love to die before it even knew our names.

I wanted you and you called me *friend*.
I brought you the apocalypse and you named
me *lover*. God is gone and Hell is raging
so where do we fit in among the chaos, between
the earthquakes quivering in our bones? I could
open you up and play your heart like a violin,

but your melody is strained, and the pitch might
summon the hounds of Hell. That is a commitment
I'm not ready for, to be dragged down in flames
before I've even baptized the destruction around
us. So dear lover of mine watch your back,
please watch your back because I have a knife
clutched in my hand and murder in my heart.

Thunderbolt

You gravitate toward me
like lightning to sand,
and the collision is the
kind of terrible beauty
that scares the birds away
and momentarily blinds
but left behind is rare glass
unique and lovely,
sharp and dangerous.

When the Hero Bleeds

We are a dam waiting to break,
caught in a choking game,
the kind where our jaws splinter
and twinge beneath an unending ocean
because the hero of our tale
eats sand

and his damsel likes
to watch him bleed for a bit,
so our rescue is delayed
by infinite grains.

The damsel finds us instead.
We applaud her cunning,
the way her orchestrated overdose
forces her hero to crawl through an empty,
hot desert. We watch together when his
seams rip and he falls apart.

From out of his torn crust
spills a new desert,
one with scarlet
grains that pulse and beat
against our skin
because when the hero bleeds we all
get caught in the sticky palpitating
of his broken heart's detonation.

Bed Sheets and Dewdrops

We buried our souls beneath night's fog
and hid our marred hearts in dewdrops
of mist. We tinted our eyes with petroleum
and burned conscience to sticky embers.

Freed from these bits of humanity,
you tied the bed sheets into a noose
and cried against my hair, your tears
falling onto my eyelashes like snowflakes.

Our hands interlocked between the scars,
and you were too close to the edge for me
to pull you back, but I could gently push
you over, one last warm touch before falling.

I made this easier. I killed you in silence
that June night and made suicide look like
murder. I saved you a final dignity and
kept you from the ridicule of whispers.

I pled guilty. Let them lock me in a cell
while they decide what to do with me.
I'll tie the bed sheets around my neck
and pull tight…tighter, until there's fog
in my eyes and I can see you again
in the reflection of my tears like dewdrops.

Dalliance

The argyle sweater he favors
is crumpled on the floor
next to his khakis, next to her
jeans where the poems he wrote
are tucked into neat squares
in her back pocket.
Her favorite is the one
he wrote about them, his
character tells her's he loves
her as his hands close around
her throat, as she chokes
on her own blood, drowning
in his crimson love. They always
murder each other in the end

because they're lava, vaporizing
life, not caring who gets in the way.
This is how destruction paints
a masterpiece -- with his smugness,
with how she makes him feel unsure
when she laughs as only one young
and cruel can. She's enigmatic,
a cross-purpose kind of ambiguity
that he isn't used to, and it's overused,
all of this, but he's sunk too far
into the depths of her to care.

So they fall like angels into Hell.
They fall, and burn, and finally
speak the cursed word of love.

Simpatico

Your word, not mine, but you called us that
and I had to write you something, didn't I?
Yes, because my heart is beating to the sacred
tune of *yours, yours, yours*, and even when it stops,
I will belong to you. You, who fills me
with poetry and madness until I cannot discern
the difference between the two, until I would
sacrifice anything for one night of you and me

and the devil's wine, a night where we could
love without sin. Though for you I'd commit
every wickedness on Earth. My silent want
aches for your pariah love, for the tragedy that
could be us. You know this. Your eyes scream
for it, and I wonder if you understand how desire
begs my tongue to skin you alive. My trembling
lips plead for you to not leave them lonely, to kiss

me just once, and sometimes you look at me like
you would, like you would shove me against
the wall and fuck away all those repressed touches
and clean words because we know our grains are
crafted from Hell's discards, and baby just embrace
this simpatico love. Do anything you want with me.

I would let you.

Breathe with me. Breathe and love
and die beside me, simpatico.
Reflect my immoral love.

Vanish

Did you think our mistakes would melt
into pavement and be whispered away
like windswept cinders?
You tell me to forget, to move on,
but I'd have to take a razor to my tongue
to forget the way your kiss tastes.

The Wrong Side of Midnight

I asked God for a bullet. He didn't reply, but the Devil sent a demon to me. I met my demon late, on the wrong side of midnight where the moon doesn't glow. He blended in with the darkness and I told him he looked like the kind of evil I would sell my soul to, like it was some sick pick-up line. He took me home and said he walked in darkness, but dreamt of light. I told him I suffered in the light and dreamt of darkness. He opened up his cold arms to me and I found serenity in a demon's embrace.

He showed me how to seize the inherent selfishness that came with being human, to make no apologies. He revealed how to love without sorrow, and how to hate without guilt. In return I gave my demon all my secrets. I shared too much, gave too much, and now I want them all back because my demon left me in the woods. He left me to wake up dead, and now I haunt every tree until they know my tune. The leaves sing with me and the rain beats against the tree bark like the way my heart would thump if it still could. My demon ate my heart.

For years I have wandered these forests and thought it would be wretched torture, but instead I am happy. I found peace under the copse of trees and contentment between the wildflowers. My demon saved me, and when at last I smiled, he came back because now I am complete. Now I understand. He earned my trust and cared for me until we were friends, danced with me until we were lovers.

Now it is my turn to watch over those lonely demons that crawl up from Hell on the Devil's orders to fix broken souls the daylight bleached into misery. Go ahead and kick your demons to the curb. I'll be watching. I'll give them a ride home, sleep with them next to my pillow, and together my demon and I will recreate those other imps. We will show them the emotions you've been shamed into hiding, and decide if you are a thing worth saving.

The next time you're out and the moon is dark and the stars are hiding, you might be walking into the wrong side of midnight where a demon waits for you. I can tell you all the ways a demon can love, but I'd rather not have to show you all the ways they can twist you inside out until your inverted flesh is sliding down to Hell.

Skull Pop

I got lost between
Crystal Head vodka
and chewing stereo wires,
trying to recreate the way
your tongue tastes like
drunken sparks against mine.

Belladonna

She's the needle
he swallowed.
Her sharp points
carved letters
onto his ribs
her name
now a permanent
engraving inside
his blood cells
to remind him
that the high
she gave
lives forever
in his veins.

Saint MurderLove

"When I wake up, please be gone, or else
you will be dead." He warned her with
those words, pleaded for his angel to run,
but she stayed, turned to ice in his arms, and
died before she could see his transformation.

Her last *I love you* tastes like day-old vomit
soaking onto his tongue. She was never his
noose, but he tied her around his neck, and
she held that space between spine and head
so tightly. Without her, his bones crumbled.

Cupid was prohibited to use arrows for his own
purpose. He was only allowed to find love for
others, not himself. When he broke the rules,
the Devil slid under his fingertips, and Cupid
wondered why everything he touched turned to ash.

Ruined love caused the wings to rot from his
pale body. He lurked in the curve of footsteps,
his eyes turned dark with the blood of night.
He waited to crawl inside the organs of lovers,
and to infect them with the flavor of misery.

He used the tips of his arrows to dig graves for
the sweethearts of the world, but then he traded
in his bow for a shotgun. With heart-shaped
bullets he rolled out a red carpet of bloody love
and invited the forlorn to run away to Hell.

Cupid kept his new pets safe before his skin
turned inside out and he became Saint MurderLove.
He whispered madness behind the necks of partners
and held the cold barrel of his gun to their temples,
leaving the symbol of hearts smoking from their brains.

He lapped up their life source as it drooled down
from the broken skulls, and carried it back to
those he had stored in Hell. Cupid smiled and
promised to keep his lonely ones forever full
as he led them to glutton on the blood of love.

80

Lawless

You're trying to write our story
as if all we did could be contained inside
      raven ink on crumpled paper,
but I know better.

I know
how our mess
      slides off
the edges, how it spills,
puddles,
and absorbs
everything like a poisonous everglade.

The greatest cause of suffering
is to love deeply,
with your whole being,
without
chance of being saved because where's
the fun in that?
      Love madly or not at all.

Such passion is a wound scratched
into you by another,
a carved out scar
that was always meant to be bitten
into your skin,
      and you have no control
over the
depth
of this mark engraved
into your shaking body like a flame's kiss.

Stop trying to control our story
      (stop trying to control me)

Let our selfish, angry love
take over,
let us ruin the world, save each other,
and sing blood ballads
until the sun burns out

and our atoms scatter
        to go and greet the stars.

Flayed Open

Our love is like a skinned rat,
ugly and exposed, secreting
the stench of pus and rot.
The grime of our deceit sticks
to the pink wrinkles of our flesh,
bared little lies that we scurry
to hide from. We seek dark corners
to conceal our inflamed eyes,
stained nails, and the flayed open
stench of what we pretend to be
behind decaying walls
in forgotten houses.

Word Famine

Your voice soaks through
my skin. Your roots
reach deep, planted
in my veins,
a virus flowing through
my head like the buzz
of too much wine, dark
and sweet, like your blood
on my lips the night
I kissed you
after pulling stitches
from your mouth,
after delicately untangling
the threads long enough
to lick the wounds
and clean away the red
before stitching
you back together
to keep you silent
because your voice
is something I want
to run away from
and crawl back toward,
to let you feed me
contradictions, good and bad,
just so long as it is your
goodness
and your corruptions
that either save or starve me.

Heaven's Ripper

I keep angels in my bed. The barbs of their
feathered wings are chained to the posts, and
I pull down their halos to keep my angels
choked against the headboard. Their strained
necks are the colors of the universe's atoms—
colors we do not yet have names for, burning
bright and dark at once, like Pandemonium's fire.

They are angels who have dabbled in Hell's
lessons. And for this I adore them. I show love
by singing hymns between blood-stained sheets.
I build bones of sinners into an altar, and shelter
under angelic wings to absolve myself of evil.
I sweat my confessions into their skin that is not
skin, but warms me in the light of forgiveness.

I decant prayers from my breath into their mouths,
slow and sweet, like crying into wine. Paradise
withdraws from their bodies, and I bring destruction
because I am the Ripper of Heaven, but I do not
abandon my angels in alleyways like whores,
entrails exposed and organs missing. Though my
tongue does leave jagged wounds across their throats.

I whisper commands into the ears of my angels.
I am a black cat tiptoeing in the dark, seeking
vermin to gnash between the points of my teeth.
I eat their grace, swallow it like honey, and curl
my body against theirs, so they understand the
way humankind is quaking and dirty, with ugly,
naked crusts and overly desperate desires.

They close their eyes when I lay next to them.
My angels don't want to see how well I sin, but
I am granted salvation in the scent of their celestial
bodies, like rosemary. I am saved by the taste of
their holy water tears that drift from white eyes to
my shuddering lips. I am caressed between their
shoulder blades where wings reach out toward me.

I bury myself between that embrace and sigh when
my knife presses the curved veins along their wings
and see exposed nerves in lilac shades. The sound of
an angel begging is the most flowered music, soft rose
petals whispering against rain, a satin melody I drown
myself in as my blade turns their feathers to silken
string and I unthread every fiber to wrap my body inside.

The Devil grants bargains, but I make promises,
sharp commitments to my angels who are not fallen,
but stolen by my selfish hands. Was I not created in
this image? Was I not made to have my taste buds
crave the melting sugared flavor of such divine
creatures? I may not keep my seraphs in a white chapel,
but I promise my twisted love is enough to go around.

The night hurts, but I make myself feel better when
I have an angel alone, when I can cut miracles into
strips and run the frayed ends against my lips, like a
kiss from a carnation. I don't want to kill my angels,
I just want to wreck the ultimate prize of the universe,
to bring something so pure and glowing down into
the dirt and dark where the rest of us dwell as rats.

We scream and murder. We hold knives to the eyes
of our lovers and demand sympathy. I want my angels
bent and cruel, scarred and aching, to have a full under-
standing of the humans they watch over because when you
are Heaven's Ripper, you better make damn sure you tear
the place up good, that you chain God to the sky and make
him watch as you crack open his angels and fill them with sin.

I Count the Feathers

I count the feathers and wonder
is all that has been loved, still loved alone?
We dream by day, but you promised night
offered cognizance, and I wait for teeth
shaped like nightmares. The incubi of terror
linger. They invite agony into the brain,
a feeling you knew all too well.

I count the feathers and listen
to the gargle, choke, breathe,
repeat of madness. Psychosis wears
a face entombed in walls, but its soul
is trapped under ticking floorboards.
Sanity may retreat from the exposure
of light, but a heart touched by insanity
is a heart set free in darkness.

I count the feathers and ask
where the rest of the nevers vanished to?
More are found inside the cemetery
where paw prints of a black cat stain
slabs of stone. Romanticism remains,
but is sliced from the reaper's pendulum.
The fates of a kingdom by the sea paint
broken seraphs, and the never found
here crashes in waves like the last spark
of wickedness reflected in the ink of your eyes.

The rest of us are lost in screams behind
red masques. We are left in October, counting
along to the decayed canto. The storm howls
upon the rain, and I listen. I hear you madly
muttering verses from your grave and I stand
beneath the sparking thunder, watching
the way hearts turn to ravens and burst
into little black slices, and I count the feathers.

Shipwrecks

I asked him to love me
with ocean and sun,
but all he gave me
were shipwrecks
under a moonless sky.

Bite like Winter

The air distrusts your movements. It shivers,
but the frigid night of your skin renews me.
My heart longs to drown in something chilling
enough to freeze the blistering pain of the sun.

Our frosted love is a ruined miracle, like fallen
angel wings plunged into the subzero. Fragments
remain. You wield them as weapons and long to
cut me open, to leave me benumbed to your touch.

Your arctic tongue entraps me into the Siberian
night, seduces with words like drifting icebergs
and skin the color of a blue moon. I am left
questioning if your bite will taste like winter.

Teeth slide against my wrist, splitting open the thin
surface. Claim my soul for night's creatures. Tear me
open until my throat bleeds a trail of rubies, and I am
twitching in your arms, dying so that I may finally live.

Charades of the Vodka Affair

Leave me alone, for fuck's sake.
Don't go.

Don't you start listening to me now
after all those warped ambiguities
because emotions are the flaw of madness,
and aren't we perfectly sane in the dark
where you spit blood on my face
and run the buds of your vodka-stained
tongue along my neck until I shut up?

This charade of love, this laughing parody
dressed up as something outwardly noble
that internally is all sharpened glass
piercing through the organ of our decisions
until we find the choice between
our vile hearts, our contradicting wants,
until we are both terminated in the end.

Predator Haunt

I will not obey the rules of this world
if it becomes devoid of you. To be emptied
of your atoms and spit and oxygen
is to have my lungs weighed with cement.

I hunt for you, for your eyes hidden
beneath frozen streams, for the pattern
of your beloved face on every burnt tree,
for the twist of your smile in the evening
clouds. I ask every bird to sing me a song
in your voice. I bite the necks of all humans
and search for the taste of you, to know
if they too have swallowed your saccharine blood.

I tear apart the world I am so fond of
just to find you again before the final
blink of the sun, before the ground
crumbles and we are disintegrated.

Devotion

You have become my omen. I pray to all the gods of the old and new worlds, say my blessings, and cross my heart to protect my loved ones from your curse. In the daylight I hide from you. When the night descends, your call sounds and keeps me from sleep. I slip away to find you, though my mind screams to stay away.

I find you, fall into your arms, my dirty drug, my satanic secret. I worship you like a cult and let you cut me open just enough for you to draw bleeding crosses on my abdomen.

When the sun rises I'll run away again, put miles between our bodies, but when the moon shines through my bedroom window, I am yours.

We speak with wet, begging tongues, and all I want is you, to take you to the altar and nail your body to the cross. Let your screams become my prayers, let me suck the marrow from your bones like forbidden fruit, and let me find salvation in your tears. Let me worship our devotion more than anything in this life.

Let me destroy you, fall apart inside your blood, and immortalize such reverent love.

Jagged Grains

You hide implications under your nails.
I peel them away to expose tiny clocks
hanging from your bones between ribbons
of flesh built up like an old cathedral.

There is time flowing backward in the gears
of your muscles and I think they have honesties
to tell me, but I don't want your truths, I know
they will slice my tongue with jagged sand grains.

When you step closer, my skeleton hisses to rip
away and leave me shriveled in the sun like shed
skin from a snake. But I still sin for you tonight,
all nights, because it's better than being alone.

Even when the seaside is torn-up and our duet
remains unfinished, we will snap necks and spines
until the mystery of the world breaks with its core
poking through the earth like ribs through a heart.

I will build a monument from your bones
and your hidden clocks, from your dried meat
and sand-veins. I want your damnation,
and I will make the wreckage beautiful.

Emetic

You asked to see my wounds,
the ones I kept hidden in the back
of my throat, perched inside
my trachea like a bear in a cave.

You told me to open up more,
to let you help, to heal me.
You wanted to make me smile,
but this was never about you.

I ripped words from my tongue
for you. I split their letters open
like eggshells until my sorrows oozed
out, a slippery yolk in your hands.

You never closed your fingers tight
enough and my burdens, the ones you
demanded to hear about, dripped
from the gaps of your loose fists.

I caught the drops in my mouth,
swallowed down the same pains until
the next time we replay this, and I repeat
the vomit-gulp-vomit of the words and hurt
you will never purge from me.

I Like Us Dead

I like us dead,
twisted around
each other's corpses
like possessive vipers,
slithering in a bed
of our own venom
until our skin bursts
in pestilential,
wild-berry shades.

I like us dead
because instead of
the weight souls bring
we just feel a slow
burn like whiskey
being poured through
our veins, and we enjoy
the way freedom tastes
like smoke rings.

Knifed

You're too easy to overdose on,
and I'm the addict injecting your
blood into my body until it makes
me itch, makes me
scratch, scratch, scratch
a hole
clean through my chest.

There pulses my beating heart,
exposed, raw, waiting
for you to slide
your blade into it, the way you have
whispered about it in your sleep,
your dreams, for weeks now.
Here I am, destroy me,
love me
stab your death straight through
my decaying bones.

Masterpiece

I want to paint you, he whispers
and I know his methods are
unconventional, but I want this,
to be immortalized in his art.
He holds an empty palette under
my forearm and cuts deeply,
drains me until the tray is filled.

He paints me as I am, strapped naked
to the chair, but on the canvas I am
rose-colored. For shading he plucks
my eyelashes out one by one and grinds
their thin blackness into a fine powder.

He yanks at my hair until my eyes water
and collects the drops to splatter around
the place where my irises will go. Strands
of my hair are positioned on his creation
with delicacy, aimed for precision in this red
adaptation of me. He rips off half of each
of the nails on my fingers and toes to place
on the smaller version. He slides a knife under
my bottom lip and skims a layer of skin off.

I am full of such bright life on the picture,
but the real me is a mess. I am a torn
disaster of a human being. When he's
finished I'm half-dead, but on the canvas
I am as complete as I ever could be. I'm
his creation, a portrait of a girl that is forever.
I am wrecked, but I am his masterpiece.

Knotted Threads

The tips of her fingers ache to dig
her nails into his pliable flesh,
to squeeze his frame until veins
burst from his trembling skin.

Her teeth crave to pull apart layers
and make enough space inside
his twisted body for her to crawl
inside the slippery red of him.

And if the darkness turns haunting,
she will hook her neck in the knotted,
lovely veins of his, and die
by the thread of what gave him life.

Swan Song

My tongue is sin-flavored
and you are edging
teeth first into my mouth,
trying to get into my veins,
but my blood is too strong
for your skin to handle.

It will intoxicate you quickly
and you'll stumble around
like a drunk seeing blurry
road lines before crashing
into the guardrail and flying
through the windshield.

After the glass shatters I will
gaze over the cliff top at your
broken body and attempt
to sing you farewell lullabies
of love, but I know my serenade
will turn into a song of suicide.

The Sin in Saint

Marry me? Saint asks Sin, his cherry flavored
lover with bourbon eyes and ash-stained lips,
but she refuses and tells this man of morals
that he does not know how to love a woman
born from the womb of evil. They have not
slept together, but he's down on one knee, ready
to sign his life over to a daughter of darkness.

He's under her heels like a dog,
laying down
without a single fight in his humble bones.
It makes her sick.

The second time Saint asks Sin to marry him,
he walks to her with palms splayed,
says he will do anything. She's his greatest scar.
He will be her savior from the Devil's grasp.

Sin tells her fool she prefers the open impiety of the Devil, the way he wears
his wrongs on his skin, rather than hiding longings under a martyr's robes
the way Saint does.

Saint gives in, embraces
his desires and names Sin his Paradise.

His tongue slips into her mouth and sucks
the taste of evil from her teeth, an addictive
flavor that drives him to hunger.

He comes to Sin with clothes soaked in the blood he now craves.

Saint lured innocents into the dark, pressed his canines
against their throats and ripped life to pieces. He stole
their souls and brought them to Sin, an offering of his
new faiths and freedom. *Marry me,* Saint asks Sin
and kisses her with blood on his lips.

She accepts.

Your Last Bullet

I tried to write you a love letter, but it turned into a list of the ways I would like to kill you.

baby, you make murder look so good

I tried to sketch your portrait, but I drew you in shades of blue. I drew you dead. Your eyes were peeled back, as if to look into your skull for one last good memory.

Someone has to walk away hurt from this. It's a rule. *The* rule. The one that signifies the finish of our story, so let's end the tale here, between you and I. The space is vast and the air cold, but our breathing leaves puffs in the air that mingle -- yours and mine.

breathe, bash your head against the wall, bleed, bleed, bleed

We surrendered ourselves to the darkness,

I am tired of morning kisses

but we don't talk about this, about what we did when the rest of the world slept, how we damned ourselves. The curves of your lips will always cause my heart to wither.
You are my muse.
My madness.

I cannot deny the way those aspects interweave and leave me in want to murder you, to draw inspiration from the metallic fragrance of your blood. Even then, you would be the ghost to haunt me across all planes of existence.

I love you because you called me poet, and you are the perfect words I will never write. You are pollution in my bloodstream, and I could rid myself of you, but I know I'll choke on my desire before I cleanse my passions. There is no pride here, no shame. Just the wrath of lust, sin combating sin for first place and damn if we didn't give it a good run with our gluttony of each other. We've become vultures, circling one another to swallow the dying scraps of love.

I'm not your happy fiction and you sure as hell are not mine.

but we keep pretending, keep lying to each other, to our selves

We both want better endings, who doesn't? If you think that means I will let you go, then you still don't understand.

I love you because when I go to slit your throat, I know you'll send a bullet to my heart.

ABOUT THE AUTHOR

Sara Tantlinger resides outside of Pittsburgh on a hill in the woods. She holds an M.F.A in Writing Popular Fiction from Seton Hill University. Some of her work can be found in publications such as Page & Spine, The Literary Hatchet, Liquid Imagination, The Five-Two, and the HWA Poetry Showcase Volume II.

When she's not writing, Sara enjoys drinking coffee, photographing graveyards, and rereading Poe for the hundredth time.

Find her at saratantlinger.wordpress.com and on Twitter @SaraJane524

The Mortuary Monster
Andrew J. Stone.

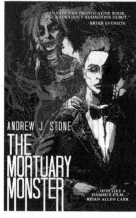

It's Corpse Bride meets Eraserhead despite Gonzalo's best efforts to live a life like Leave It to Beaver's. Gonzalo grew up in the cemetery under the care of his monstrous parents and in the company of decaying corpses. As a result, he only desired one thing throughout his childhood: To be normal enough to join society. But despite his attempts at running away from his family, he has never been able to leave the mortuary. Now, as an adult, Gonzalo manages the cemetery. His family has died yet he is still unable to leave. Then, on the night of the annual Cadaver Tea party, something impossible happens—he impregnates the corpse Fiona. In an attempt to normalize the cemetery before his child's birth, Gonzalo begins to close all the coffins, forever locking the dead inside. Without the intercession of corpses like Henry, the voluntary babysitter of abused children, Lionel, the life-long explorer, Victoria, the world's first professional deep-sea water ski champion, and Vincent, Victoria's long-time lover and trainer, Gonzalo believes he and Fiona will be able to raise their child to join the rest of the world. But in the throes of terminal calcium deficiency, Fiona's bones deteriorate to dust immediately after she gives birth. Can Gonzalo make the young Frank, his now motherless, half-corpse son, normal enough for society? Can he raise his son without becoming like his own parents? Will Gonzalo become the Mortuary Monster he has spent his whole life trying to escape?

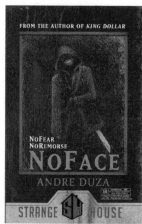

NoFace
Andre Duza

Erin Hopkins has a secret admirer. It could be anyone... Her boyfriend Paul... Her strange new friend Lea... One of her classmates at the university... Or maybe it's the hooded figure with the ghastly smile that's been haunting her dreams of late. The same one who saved her that night, one month ago, when she was nearly raped on her way home from work. As Erin struggles to put her life back together, she soon discovers a connection to the infamous federal research facility, the Koechner Institute, and to a blind, sword-wielding assassin born of clandestine government experimentation. Something twisted has come to suburbia. And it has a few scores to settle.

Available at Strangehouseonline.com and Amazon!

Made in the USA
San Bernardino, CA
09 February 2017